Brimming with creative inspiration, how-to projects, and useful information to enrich your everyday life, Quarto Knows is a favorite destination for those pursuing their interests and passions. Visit our site and dig deeper with our books into your area of interest: Quarto Creates, Quarto Cooks, Quarto Homes, Quarto Lives, Quarto Drives, Quarto Explores, Quarto Gifts, or Quarto Kids.

Text © 2021 Barbara Taylor
Illustrations © 2021 Stephen Collins

First Published in 2021 by Frances Lincoln Children's Books,
an imprint of The Quarto Group.
100 Cummings Center, Suite 265D, Beverly, MA 01915, USA.
T +1 978-282-9590 F +1 078-283-2742 www.QuartoKnows.com

The right of Stephen Collins to be identified as the illustrator and Barbara Taylor to be identified as the author of this work has been asserted by them in accordance with the Copyright, Designs and Patents Act, 1988 (United Kingdom).

A CIP record for this book is available from the Library of Congress.

ISBN 978-0-7112-5637-8

The illustrations were created digitally on a tablet computer using watercolor brushes, with calligraphy brushes and pencils for the details.
Set in Futura

Published by Katie Cotton
Commissioned by Lucy Brownridge
Designed by Karissa Santos
Edited by Hannah Dove
Production by Dawn Cameron
Fact checked by Professor Mike Benton

Manufactured in Guangdong, China EB012021

9 8 7 6 5 4 3 2 1

MIX
Paper from
responsible sources
FSC® C124385

THE DINOSAUR AWARDS

Written by Barbara Taylor

Illustrated by Stephen Collins

Frances Lincoln
Children's Books

WELCOME TO
THE DINOSAUR AWARDS!

Roll up, roll up! The ceremony is about to begin—and you're invited. We're here to celebrate some downright dazzling dinosaurs, and shine a spotlight on their finest features and unique qualities. We'll be awarding prizes for the bushiest tail, the biggest bite, the longest neck, and much more. You'll encounter some familiar faces and discover some lesser-known dinosaurs, too.

Meet the predator with an Elvis Presley hairstyle. Learn about the speedy dinosaur who could run as fast as a racehorse, and the famous herbivore known as the "Unicorn dinosaur." Find out what makes them each so prizeworthy and discover how they lived their lives.

It's been a tricky task choosing the winners, but we hope you approve and find plenty to marvel at in this treasury of talented dinosaurs.

Now, put your hands together and clap!
The Dinosaur Awards is about to begin...

The Winners of The Dinosaur Awards are:

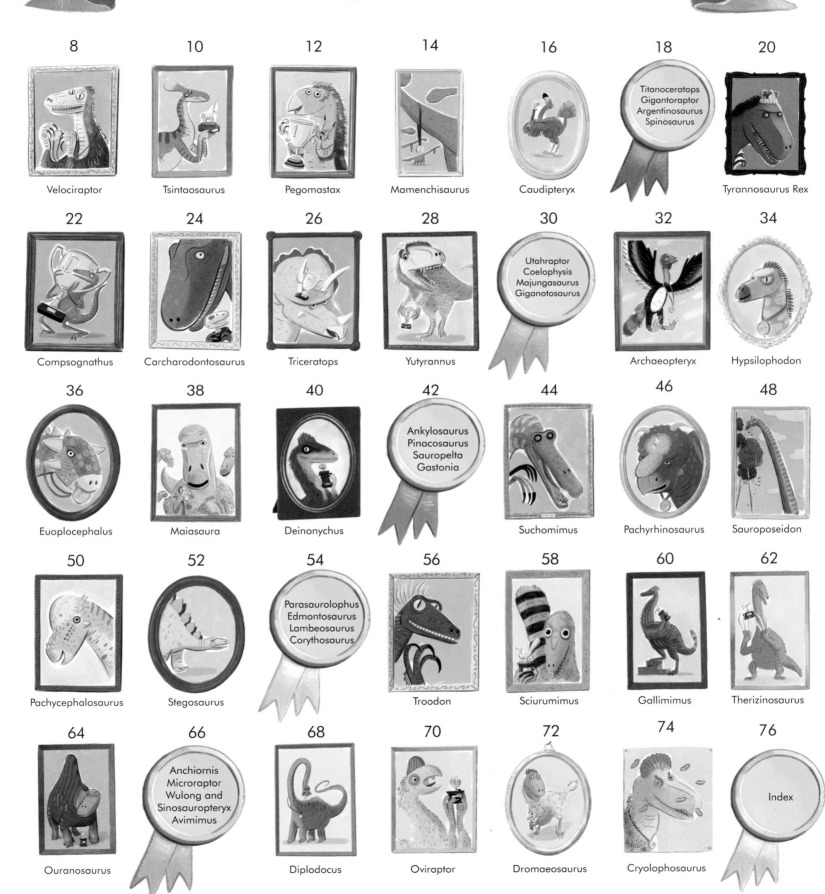

8 Velociraptor

10 Tsintaosaurus

12 Pegomastax

14 Mamenchisaurus

16 Caudipteryx

18 Titanoceratops Gigantoraptor Argentinosaurus Spinosaurus

20 Tyrannosaurus Rex

22 Compsognathus

24 Carcharodontosaurus

26 Triceratops

28 Yutyrannus

30 Utahraptor Coelophysis Majungasaurus Giganotosaurus

32 Archaeopteryx

34 Hypsilophodon

36 Euoplocephalus

38 Maiasaura

40 Deinonychus

42 Ankylosaurus Pinacosaurus Sauropelta Gastonia

44 Suchomimus

46 Pachyrhinosaurus

48 Sauroposeidon

50 Pachycephalosaurus

52 Stegosaurus

54 Parasaurolophus Edmontosaurus Lambeosaurus Corythosaurus

56 Troodon

58 Sciurumimus

60 Gallimimus

62 Therizinosaurus

64 Ouranosaurus

66 Anchiornis Microraptor Wulong and Sinosauropteryx Avimimus

68 Diplodocus

70 Oviraptor

72 Dromaeosaurus

74 Cryolophosaurus

76 Index

VELOCIRAPTOR

How to say the name:
Vel-OSS-ee-rap-tor
Meaning: speedy robber
When it lived:
74–70 MYA Cretaceous Period

Found in: Asia (Mongolia, China)
Diet: reptiles, amphibians, insects, baby dinosaurs, mammals
Length: 6 ft
Height: up to 2 ft 7 in
Weight: up to 33 lbs

The real Velociraptor was very different from the movie stars of *Jurassic Park*. It was small, covered in feathers, and not quite as cunning or clever. But it did have tremendous talons (sharp, hooked claws on its feet), which made it a menacing hunter that would have starred in smaller creatures' nightmares.

This turkey-sized predator was a fast runner, living up to the first part of its name, which means "speedy." It ran after small mammals and reptiles, flicking forward its two huge, hooked toe talons at the last minute to stab its prey and pin it to the ground. An eagle uses its strong talons like this today. Unlike an eagle, Velociraptor had a mouthful of very sharp, pointy teeth, with jagged edges. It also had three smaller curved claws on each arm, which helped it to stop its victims from escaping.

Despite having feathers and winglike arms, Velociraptor could not fly or glide. Instead, its shorter, fluffier feathers helped to keep its body warm.

Velociraptor had a fairly large brain for its size, so it was quite a smart little dinosaur, although no genius.

The **TERRIBLY TALON-TED** *Award*

This nimble, birdlike dinosaur used terrifying hooked talons on its toes to capture its prey.

Oh my gosh I love your nails...

NAIL BAR

They're so long and strong... you could kill with them!

Are they natural?

Yes—I'm lucky...

It runs in my species!

A Velociraptor's teeth were replaced throughout its life, so they were always fresh, sharp, and ready for a vicious attack.

A Velociraptor had large eyes and would have been able to see well. Some scientists think this keen eyesight may have helped it hunt at night.

Its teeth curved backward to stop prey escaping from its jaws!

Velociraptor moved on two legs. It could reach speeds of up to 37 mph—much faster than top human sprinters. When it walked or ran, it held its two really big toe claws off the ground, probably to keep them nice and sharp.

TSINTAOSAURUS

How to say the name:
SIN-tow-SORE-us
Meaning: Tsingtao lizard
When it lived:
83–71 MYA Cretaceous Period

Found in: Asia (China)
Diet: pine needles, cycads
Length: 33 ft
Height: 12 ft
Weight: 3 tons

Were unicorns alive and well in dinosaur times? Well, when scientists first discovered the fossilized bones of Tsintaosaurus, they thought it had a tall bony spike sticking out of its forehead, so it soon became known as the "Unicorn dinosaur."

Scientists can now show, however, that this spike probably pointed backward and formed part of a hollow head crest. This may have looked like the head crests of a group of dinosaurs called "duck-bills," which are named after their wide, ducklike snouts. Tsintaosaurus was probably an older ancestor of these duck-billed dinosaurs.

Unlike a duck, Tsintaosaurus had hundreds of teeth lining the jaws behind its beak. Tsintaosaurus used its sharp beak to snip the leaves from plants, then chewed them to a mushy pulp with its teeth. When these teeth wore down with all the hard work of chomping and grinding, sharp new gnashers popped out to replace them.

The **UNICORN** *Award*

Tsintaosaurus's headgear might have looked more like a shoehorn than a unicorn horn, but we still think it's a legendary dinosaur.

THE UNICORN AWARD GOES TO TSINTAOSAURUS

Peaceful, plant-eating Tsintaosaurus probably lived in herds. Many pairs of eyes in the herd could keep a lookout for any danger.

Some scientists thought that Tsintaosaurus's spike was just a nose bone or a skull bone that had moved out of place. They did not believe that the bone belonged on top of its head at all.

Tsintaosaurus weighed 3 tons. That's about four times as heavy as a cow.

Tsintaosaurus could walk on either two legs or four legs. This allowed it to feed at different heights and eat a variety of different plants, from ferns growing near the ground to needles higher up on conifer tree branches.

Scientists think that the "unicorn horn" was probably part of a large crest that was joined to the front of the snout at one end and projected from the top of the skull at the other end.

Tsintaosaurus may have used its crest to call to its friends and relatives. The crest may also have helped individuals within a herd to identify each other. Birds such as cockatoos have crests, which they use to show off and attract mates. Maybe Tsintaosaurus did, too.

PEGOMASTAX

How to say the name:
PEG-oh-MASS-tax
Meaning: strong jaw
When it lived:
200–190 MYA Jurassic Period

Found in: Africa (South Africa)
Diet: leaves, seeds, nuts, fruit
Length: 2 ft
Height: less than 2 ft
Weight: less than 5 lbs

Imagine a dinosaur the size of a cat, with fangs like Dracula, a beak like a parrot, a bristly back like a porcupine, and a bad attitude: meet the Pegomastax!

Although this strange little punk had fangs like a vampire, it was not a blood-sucking monster at all. It was, in fact, a veggie dinosaur. It probably used its cool jagged fangs for slashing and nipping at enemies, competing with rivals to win a mate, or even digging for food. Behind its fangs, Pegomastax had tall teeth, which worked like a pair of self-sharpening scissors to slice up plants and fruit.

Pegomastax is one of the smallest dinosaurs ever discovered, so it would have been vulnerable to attack by the fierce predators of the Jurassic world. But Pegomastax was no wet blanket! The tough bristles on its head and back would have made it look bigger than it really was and far less appetizing—after all, what predator wants an itchy, scratchy, fang-tastic snack?

Its strong jaws and a stiff, parrotlike beak made cracking and crushing food easy for Pegomastax: the ultimate hard nut.

The
PINT-SIZED PUNK
Award

This dino might be small and cute, but its sharp beak and spiky attitude make it a perfect prehistoric punk.

THE PINT-SIZED PUNK AWARD GOES TO PEGOMASTAX

The fossilized remains of Pegomastax were hidden away and forgotten in the store rooms of an American university for nearly 50 years.

Eventually, a scientist called Paul Sereno started to work on the fossils. They were found in rock that was about 200 million years old.

He pieced together the fragments and studied them closely, eventually discovering a fanged dinosaur that certainly didn't need to dress up for a Halloween party!

Pegomastax had two pointed fangs in its lower jaw, making it look frightening. When Pegomastax closed its mouth, these fangs fitted neatly into pockets on the opposite jaw, so they didn't show.

The punky bristles on the head and back of a Pegomastax may have been different colors, helping these dinosaurs to identify friends or attract mates.

If Pegomastax was attacked, its best form of defense was to run away quickly on its long back legs.
If it was cornered by a predator, it would probably have used its fangs to fight for its survival.

MAMENCHISAURUS

How to say the name:
Mah-MEN-chi-SORE-us
Meaning: Mamen Stream lizard
When it lived:
160–145 MYA Jurassic Period

Found in: Asia (Mongolia, China)
Diet: conifers, ferns, cycads, mosses, horsetails
Length: 69–115 ft
Height: 30–36 ft
Weight: 20–35 tons

With a neck as long as the average city bus, Mamenchisaurus is head and shoulders above the rest, and easily wins this award!

In fact, Mamenchisaurus's neck was up to about 45 ft long, which is a whopping EIGHT times longer than a giraffe's neck. Experts think that Mamenchisaurus probably held its neck fairly straight because the joints between the bones made it stiff and not very flexible.

To gobble up low-growing plants, Mamenchisaurus probably stood still to save energy and swept its neck back and forth close to the ground. It would have also been able to poke its head a long way into dense forests or wetlands to reach tasty plants such as ferns, mosses, and horsetails. Its peglike teeth were ideal for stripping large mouthfuls of leaves off branches.

Nearly everything about this dinosaur was supersized, including its diet! Mamenchisaurus had to eat enormous quantities of plant food every day just to keep up its energy and stay alive. It was so heavy it would have sunk if it had tried to walk on soft, spongy ground. The only part of Mamenchisaurus that wasn't ginormous was its brain, which was teeny tiny!

Mamenchisaurus probably lived in herds, much like its long-necked relatives, Diplodocus and Argentinosaurus.

Supporting the extremely stretched-out neck of a Mamenchisaurus were 19 hollow and lightweight neck bones; a giraffe has only seven neck bones!

At the end of its tail, Mamenchisaurus had a small bony club, which might have helped this dinosaur to defend itself from predators as it whipped its tail from side to side.

Like an elephant, Mamenchisaurus had thick pads on its heels to cushion the great weight of its body. It was a slow-mover, strolling steadily along at no more than 8 mph.

CAUDIPTERYX

How to say the name:
Caw-DIP-ter-ix
Meaning: tail feather
When it lived:
130–123 MYA Cretaceous Period

Found in: Asia (China)
Diet: plants, insects
Length: 3 ft
Height: 2–3 ft
Weight: 15 lbs 7 oz

Is it a bird? Is it a plane? Is it a dino-bird? No, it's Caudipteryx! This little dinosaur boasted many birdlike features and may have developed from early birdlike dinosaurs, such as Archaeopteryx.

One of these birdlike features was a dazzling plume of feathers on its tail. It's possible that Caudipteryx may have fanned these feathers out and strutted around to show off to mates, a bit like a peacock does today.

Like early birds, Caudipteryx also had small, weak, spiky teeth, which pointed outward in the front of its top jaw. Its lower jaw was toothless and may have ended in a horny beak.

Despite all the similarities, there was one common bird skill that Caudipteryx never mastered—flight! Instead, Caudipteryx whizzed around on its two long, strong legs. Its arm feathers may have helped it to steer while it was running fast.

The **PROUD AS A PEACOCK** *Award*

Caudipteryx was like a bird because of its feathers, small beaked head, short tail, and birdlike feet. It may have evolved from birds that lost the ability to fly.

THE PROUD AS A PEACOCK AWARD GOES TO CAUDIPTERYX

Caudipteryx was one of the first feathered dinosaurs to be discovered. It had short, fluffy feathers covering its body like a warm comforter.

On its arms, Caudipteryx had one row of long feathers, which linked together and were similar to the feathers of modern flightless birds.

At the tip of its tail, Caudipteryx had more feathers, which were each about 8 in long. Fossil feathers show bands of dark and light, which may mean that the feathers had colored stripes.

Caudipteryx may have used its tail fan for displaying to mates, or possibly for steering when it was running along very fast.

Living beside the lakes and rivers of China, Caudipteryx would have fed mostly on plants, but snapped up any insects that were common in these wetland habitats. It would have swallowed whole any small prey it managed to catch.

Its diet would have been difficult to digest, but Caudipteryx had a trick up its sleeve—it swallowed small stones, which helped grind up the food in its stomach.

The BIG IS BEAUTIFUL Awards

Roll out the red carpet, it's time for the Big is Beautiful Awards. Let's discover some of the most gigantic, humongous, and extraordinarily ENORMOUS dinosaurs discovered so far.

TITANOCERATOPS (Tie-TAN-oh-SER-a-tops)
The Supersized Skull Award

Length: 22 ft; **Weight:** 7 tons
When it lived: 83–70 MYA Cretaceous Period
Found in: North America

This huge ancestor of Triceratops was named "titanic horn face," after the Titans (a group of giant, immortal gods in Greek mythology). Titanoceratops had an enormous skull, which was 8 ft 6 in long. That's about as long as two eight-year-olds standing on top of each other!

GIGANTORAPTOR (Jie-GAN-toe-rap-tor)
The Big Bird Award

Length: 26 ft; **Weight:** 1.5 tons
When it lived: 85–79 MYA Cretaceous Period
Found in: Asia (Mongolia)

Looking a bit like an over-sized ostrich, Gigantoraptor was the largest known beaked dinosaur and the largest feathered dinosaur yet discovered. It was probably an omnivore, using its strong, snapping beak to feed on plants, bugs, eggs, and small animals and its long claws to pull leaves and fruit from trees. To escape predators, Gigantoraptor probably ran very fast on its long, powerful legs.

ARGENTINOSAURUS (Ar-GEN-tee-no-SORE-us)
The Heavyweight Herbivore Award

Length: 72–114 ft; **Weight:** 73–85 tons
When it lived: 100–92 MYA Cretaceous Period
Found in: South America (Argentina)

Weighing perhaps as much as six fire engines, this heavyweight dinosaur would have made the ground shake as it strolled slowly along. It needed to eat and digest vast quantities of plants just to keep its enormous body going. Scientists can't be sure of its exact size as only some parts of its skeleton have ever been found, such as ribs, spine, and leg bones.

SPINOSAURUS (SPINE-oh-SORE-us)
The Colossal Carnivore Award

Length: 39–59 ft; **Weight:** 9–20 tons
When it lived: 95–70 MYA Cretaceous Period
Found in: North Africa

One of the biggest meat-eating dinosaurs discovered so far, Spinosaurus ate big fish and sea reptiles and may have been able to swim. The huge skin-covered sail on its back was supported by extra-long spine bones, which were at least 5 ft 4 in long. Fat may have been stored in the sail and used as weight to keep the dinosaur swimming underwater. Other theories are that the sail helped to control body temperature, or that skin patterns on the sail helped individuals to identify each other, or display to potential mates.

TYRANNOSAURUS REX (T. REX)

How to say the name:
Tie-RAN-oh-SORE-us Rex
Meaning: tyrant lizard king
When it lived:
68–66 MYA Cretaceous Period

Found in: North America
Diet: other dinosaurs, alive or dead
Length: 39 ft
Height: 13 ft
Weight: up to 9 tons

The
The
KING OF THE DINOSAURS
Award

With a bone-crushing bite, over 50 banana-sized, serrated teeth and jaws big enough to swallow a person whole, the famous T. rex definitely deserves to win the award for the King of the Dinosaurs!

The incredible force of T.rex's bite was much more powerful than the bite of any other land animal that has ever lived. Thick neck muscles supported its huge skull, which was up to 5 feet long. Inside its skull, a T.rex's brain was almost twice as big as that of other giant, meat-eating dinosaurs and had large areas devoted to seeing and smelling.

T. rex's talents don't end there! If people had lived at the same time as the dinosaurs, it would have been almost impossible to escape from a T. rex by running away. It's thought that T. rex might have chased after its prey at speeds of up to 25 mph.

The jury is still out on whether T. rex was covered in scales or feathers. T. rex babies probably had fluffy feathers to keep them warm and adults may have had bristly feathers in a few places.

As long as a bus, T. rex was one of the largest meat-eating dinosaurs that ever lived.

Tell me again why you love me so?

Your brain's the biggest!

Your teeth are the sharpest!

You run so fast!

Um...

You look fab in feathers?!

T. rex's eyeballs were bigger than a tennis ball! The eyes looked more to the front than to the sides. This helped T. rex to look forward to see its prey and judge distances well.

The long tail of a T. rex had a thick, muscular base, which helped to counterbalance its heavy body. The tail sometimes had as many as 40 bones inside to provide shape and support.

The bite of a T. rex was three times more powerful than that of a saltwater crocodile. It could probably tear over 440 lbs of flesh from its victims in a single brutal bite.

The arms of a T. rex were just over 3 ft long, but were strong enough to grab and hold struggling prey while this fierce dinosaur ate it alive!

COMPSOGNATHUS

How to say the name:
Komp-SOG-nay-thuss
Meaning: pretty jaw
When it lived:
155–145 MYA Jurassic Period

Found in: Europe (Germany, France)
Diet: insects, lizards, fish, frogs, snails
Length: 2–4 ft 7 in
Height: 1 ft
Weight: 6 lbs 6 oz

One of the smallest of all dinosaurs, teeny Compsognathus was no bigger than a modern-day chicken. But it was one fiesty piece of work!

This tiny terror was a fierce and agile predator. It ran very quickly on its tip-toes, holding its long tail off the ground for balance. This tail worked like the rudder on a boat, allowing Compsognathus to change direction suddenly as it chased after its prey.

It may have been small in stature, but Compsognathus showed no mercy. It used its three-clawed hands to grasp its unlucky prey and its sharp teeth to bite into larger victims. Its long, flexible neck helped it to reach out in all directions to snatch its victims before they could escape.

There is no fossil evidence so far that Compsognathus hunted in packs, but often, small dinosaurs like this worked in groups to keep safe and take down larger prey. Compsognathus may have had short, featherlike bristles on its scaly body, like those of its close relatives.

Compsognathus used its keen eyesight and nifty turn of speed to catch its meals. Small animals would have been swallowed whole.

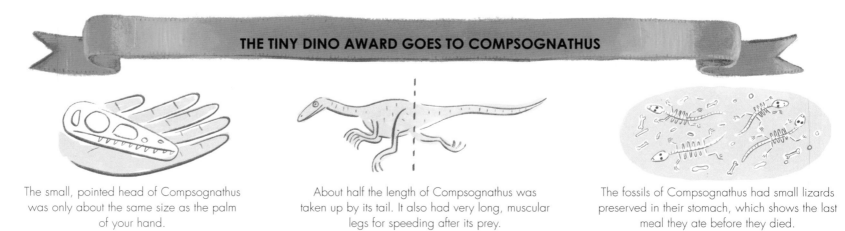

THE TINY DINO AWARD GOES TO COMPSOGNATHUS

The small, pointed head of Compsognathus was only about the same size as the palm of your hand.

About half the length of Compsognathus was taken up by its tail. It also had very long, muscular legs for speeding after its prey.

The fossils of Compsognathus had small lizards preserved in their stomach, which shows the last meal they ate before they died.

The first dinosaurs to run around on our planet, such as *Herrerasaurus, Eoraptor,* and *Panphagia,* were small, nimble hunters, which looked a bit like *Compsognathus.* They lived about 80 million years before "Compy," though.

Compsognathus may have had simple feathers on parts of its body. These probably helped to keep this tiny dino warm, but they were not suitable for flying.

Compsognathus had hollow bones, like modern-day birds. This made its skeleton very lightweight, which helped it to zoom along swiftly. Its top speed was probably up to 40 mph.

Compsognathus may have sometimes caught fish or fed on baby pterosaurs (flying reptiles), which lived in its wetland habitat.

CARCHARODONTOSAURUS

How to say the name:
Kar-ka-ro-DON-toe-SORE-us
Meaning: shark-toothed lizard
When it lived:
100–94 MYA Cretaceous Period

Found in: North Africa
Diet: plant-eating dinosaurs
Length: 26–46 ft
Height: 13 ft
Weight: 6–8 tons

The **HUGE HEAD** *Award*

Carcharodontosaurus was one big-headed dino. Its skull could measure just over 5 ft—that's about the same length as a bathtub!

A masssive meat-eater that moved on long, powerful back legs, Carcharodontosaurus looked a lot like T. rex. It lived before T. rex and also on a different continent, so Carcharodontosaurus never had to worry about T. rex stealing its food (or its thunder). It did, however, have to compete with other predators, such as Spinosaurus, which roamed the swamps and forests of North Africa at the same time. Carcharodontosaurus was almost as big as Spinosaurus and might have been able to steal and scavenge its kills.

Carcharodontosaurus was named after its jagged, triangular teeth, which looked like the teeth of a great white shark, only bigger. With these razor-sharp gnashers, Carcharodontosaurus could easily slice through the tough skin of giant plant-eating dinosaurs.

This prehistoric killer relied on its sharp senses to help it hunt. Its powerful sense of smell would have helped it to sniff out dead and rotting animals to eat.

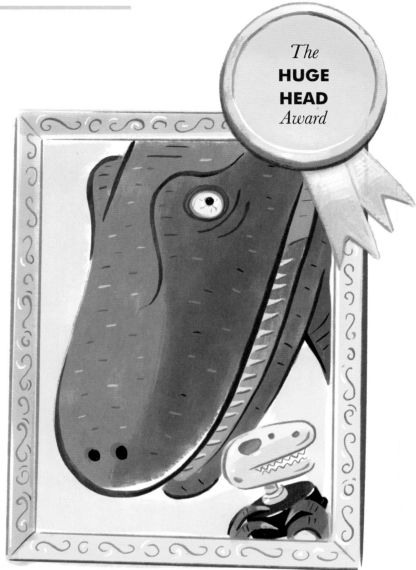

One of the biggest and most fearsome predators in Africa, Carcharodontosaurus was a powerful dinosaur, with deadly teeth and a humongous head.

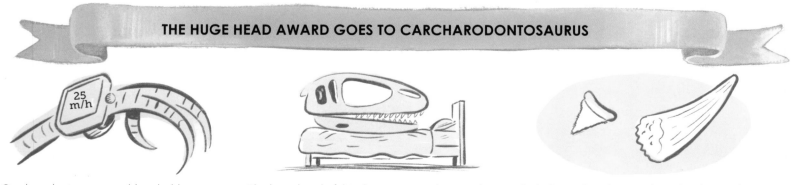

THE HUGE HEAD AWARD GOES TO CARCHARODONTOSAURUS

Carcharodontosaurus could probably run at up to 25 mph—as fast as a T. rex.

The huge head of this dinosaur was almost as long as an average single bed!

Its knife-sized teeth were about 8 in long, whereas the biggest teeth of a great white shark are only about 2 in long.

Carcharodontosaurus may have kicked its prey with its powerful legs and sharp claws, as well as biting its victims. Large arm claws helped this deadly predator to keep a firm grip on its prey.

The first fossils of this dinosaur to be found were destroyed when a museum in Munich, Germany was bombed during World War II.

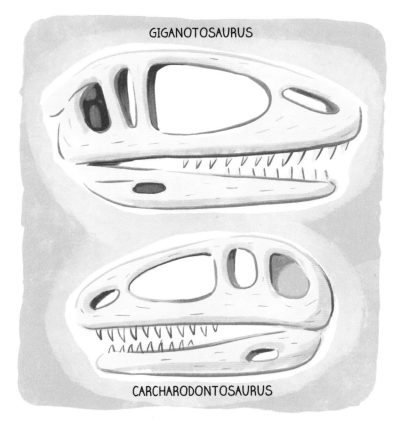

GIGANOTOSAURUS

CARCHARODONTOSAURUS

The giant Giganotosaurus dinosaur of South America is a close relative of Carcharodontosaurus. Giganotosaurus had an even larger skull than Carcharodontosaurus.

Carcharodontosaurus probably had very good eyesight, which would have helped it to hunt for its prey.

TRICERATOPS

How to say the name:
Tri-SERRA-tops
Meaning: three-horned face
When it lived:
68–66 MYA Cretaceous Period

Found in: North America
Diet: tough plants, such as ferns, cycads, and conifers
Length: 29 ft 6 in
Height: 10 ft
Weight: 5–10 tons

One of the largest and best known of the horned dinosaurs, greedy Triceratops had THREE horns: two long, pointy, bony horns, and a smaller nose horn. All three horns were covered by keratin—the material that our hair and fingernails are made of.

Triceratops's horns grew out of its massive skull, which was over 6 ft long. Fixed to the back of the skull was a short, solid neck frill made of bone, covered with thin skin and decorated with pointed studs around the edge. This snazzy shield probably protected Triceratops's neck from attack, but it could also have changed color to signal to mates, warn of danger, or help individuals recognize or fight each other. It may even have helped to regulate Triceratops's temperature.

Triceratops wandered across the marshes and forests of North America about 67 million years ago, just before the dinosaurs died out. It grazed on plants, plucking them with its sharp, parrotlike beak, which grew all through its life.

This mighty dinosaur had powerful jaws with huge muscles and rows and rows of scissorlike teeth. In fact, Triceratops had up to 800 teeth! When they became old or worn out, new teeth would replace them.

The **HUMONGOUS HORNS** *Award*

Triceratops was at least five times heavier than a bison, which is the heaviest land animal in North America today.

Hey, you'll never guess the great deal I got today!

Oh yeah?

THREE horns for the price of one!

But...you've already got three horns!

Not this kind!

Triceratops was so strong that it may have knocked down trees to reach the leaves, a bit like African elephants do today.

A big male Triceratops may have weighed almost as much as a T. rex!

Bits of a Triceratops have been found in T. rex's poop, so we know that T. rex sometimes ate Triceratops. Bite marks show that T. rex sometimes even bit through Triceratops's horns!

Scientists are not sure if Triceratops lived alone or in small groups. Fossils of a group of juvenile (young) Triceratops have been found together, so they may have lived and traveled together for protection when they were young.

YUTYRANNUS

How to say the name:
YOO-tie-RAN-us
Meaning: feathered tyrant
When it lived:
130–125 MYA Cretaceous Period

Found in: Asia (China)
Diet: other dinosaurs, alive or dead
Length: 29–33 ft
Height: 10 ft
Weight: 1–2 tons

The first huge dinosaur to be found with fuzzy feathers preserved around its fossil skeleton, Yutyrannus was named after the Mandarin word for feather, "Yu."

Yutyrannus wore its long, wispy feathers like a soft, downy overcoat, which probably covered its body from head to toe. The feathers may have looked something like the shaggy feather plumes of today's flightless birds, such as emus or cassowaries. Yutyrannus was much too big and heavy to fly. However, its feathers probably helped to control its body temperature or keep its eggs warm. They may also have been used for camouflage.

Don't be deceived by all that fluffy dino-fuzz, though! Yutyrannus was definitely NOT a big softie. It was a fierce and furious predator with a huge mouth full of about 56 sharp, banana-shaped teeth. Its skull alone was almost 3 ft long!

Scientists know very little about how Yutyrannus hunted its prey. It did run along on two legs, although it had shorter legs than a T. rex, so probably didn't run as fast.

The **FUZZY AND FURIOUS** *Award*

Would you like to meet the biggest feathered beast ever to have lived on our planet?

THE FUZZY AND FURIOUS AWARD GOES TO YUTYRANNUS

Yutyrannus was an ancestor of its famous royal relative, T. rex, but would only have reached up to T. rex's chest.

T. rex was about six times heavier than Yutyrannus!

Yutyrannus had longer arms and claws than T. rex, which may have helped it to catch its prey.

Yutyrannus had a nose crest, which it probably used to attract a mate, and to identify its friends and relatives.

Living in shady forests in a cool climate, Yutyrannus probably found its warm feather coat very useful, especially in winter.

Its feathers were 6 to 8 in long and looked a bit like the fuzzy down of baby chicks.

Yutyrannus may have used its large feet to pin down its prey while it tore off chunks of meat with its jagged teeth.

The DEADLIEST DINOSAURS Awards

Hot off the press... the winners of the Deadliest Dinosaur Awards have just been announced! These villains were truly terrifying predators back in dinosaur times and they still scare us silly today.

UTAHRAPTOR *(YOO-tah-rap-tor)*
The Colossal Claws Award

Length: 16–23 ft; **Weight:** 0.5–1 tons
When it lived: 112–100 MYA Cretaceous Period
Found in: North America

With an enormous hooked claw on its second toes, Utahraptor was one enemy you wouldn't want to make. This dangerous predator weighed as much as a polar bear and probably used its colossal, needle-sharp claws for slashing, stabbing, and even pulling out the insides of its victims. Yuck! Its award-winning claws were about 1 ft long.

COELOPHYSIS *(See-LOW-fie-sis)*
The Pack Power Award

Length: 6–9 ft 8 in; **Weight:** 40–60 lbs
When it lived: 225–190 MYA Triassic Period
Found in: Southern Africa, North America, Asia (China)

An agile, long-legged dinosaur, Coelophysis and its pack worked as a team to chase and overpower larger dinosaurs to eat for supper. It also sprinted after prey such as insects and lizards at speeds of up to 20 mph. It held its long tail up in the air to balance the weight of the front part of its body. Despite its small size, Coelophysis was a ferocious enemy, with large, sharp, jagged teeth and grasping claws.

MAJUNGASAURUS *(Mah-JOON-gah-SORE-us)*
The Cunning Cannibal Award

Length: 19 ft 7 in; **Weight:** 2 tons
When it lived: 84–71 MYA Cretaceous Period
Found in: Africa (Madagascar)

The beastliest beast ever to have existed on the African island of Madagascar, this stocky dinosaur was a top predator that sometimes turned into a cannibal. Tooth marks on Majungasaurus bones show that it even ate its own kind. Scientists are not sure, however, if the dinosaur's family and friends were alive or dead when they appeared on the dinner table. Gulp!

GIGANOTOSAURUS *(Gig-a-no-toe-SORE-us)*
The Dinosaur Killer Award

Length: 39–42 ft 6 in; **Weight:** 8–14 tons
When it lived: 99–97 MYA Cretaceous Period
Found in: South America (Argentina)

A fully paid up member of the deadliest dinosaur club, Giganotosaurus was bigger and faster than T. rex. The vast jaws of Giganotosaurus were full of almost 80 sharp teeth, each longer than an adult person's hand! Not one to be intimidated, Giganotosaurus probably hunted plant-eating dinosaurs even bigger than itself.

ARCHAEOPTERYX

How to say the name:
AR-kee-OP-ter-ix
Meaning: ancient feather
When it lived:
150–147 MYA Jurassic Period

Found in: Europe (Germany)
Diet: fish, seashore animals
Length: 1–2 ft
Height: 8 in
Weight: 1 lb 7 oz–2 lbs 2 oz

The **FIRST FLIGHT** *Award*

Scientists think Archaeopteryx was a bird-like dinosaur about the size of a pigeon. Although Archaeopteryx could fly for short distances, it wasn't very good, and it was probably a bit of a bumpy flight!

Archaeopteryx had long arms covered in well-developed flight feathers similar to those of modern pigeons. Unlike modern birds however, Archaeopteryx had a skeleton like that of a small Velociraptor, teeth in its slim, pointed jaws instead of a beak, sharp claws on its fingers and toes, and a 20 inch-long, stiff tail.

Archaeopteryx was a triple threat: it could fly (a bit), it could run, using its tail to balance, and it could probably also swim. These skills would have been useful because it lived on dry, wooded islands on the edge of a warm, shallow sea.

Archaeopteryx may have plucked fish from the salty seawaters, or snapped up crabs, shellfish, worms, and insects. Archaeopteryx had about 50 small, pointy teeth in its jaws, which were ideal for snapping up its small animal prey. It may have used its sharp "killer" claws to pin down larger prey.

Archaeopteryx probably flew for short distances by flapping its wings, a bit like a modern pheasant. This would have helped it to hunt for prey or escape predators.

Archaeopteryx had a V-shaped "wishbone" in its shoulder girdle, which provided strength to the chest when it was flying. Wishbones are formed by the two collar bones joining together. They are found in modern birds such as chickens.

The Jurassic skies high above Archaeopteryx were dominated by huge flying reptiles, called pterosaurs, which were only distantly related to Archaeopteryx. Pterosaur wings were made of skin but they had small fluffy feathers on their head, body, and legs, which helped to keep them warm.

Archaeopteryx held its big second toe claw off the ground. This probably helped to keep the tip of the claw sharp for attacking prey.

HYPSILOPHODON

How to say the name:
HIP-sil-OH-foe-don
Meaning: high-ridge tooth
When it lived:
125–120 MYA Cretaceous Period
Found in: North America, Europe

Diet: low-growing plants, such as conifers and ferns
Length: 7 ft 7 in
Height: 3 ft
Weight: 44–110 lbs

Hypsilophodon ran extremely fast on its long back legs. This champion escape artist could twist, turn, duck, weave, and bob as it ran along to evade attackers.

Hypsilophodon had a small head, which was no bigger than a human hand. Inside its mouth were rows of razor-sharp teeth, which could be replaced when they were old or worn. These chisel-like teeth were used to slice up food. Hypsilophodon was an unusual dinosaur because it had pointed front teeth as well as a sharp beak. (Most dinosaurs with beaklike mouths had no front teeth.) Hypsilophodon also had muscular cheek pouches where it could store its food while chewing, like hamsters, or possibly carry the food to a safe place if danger threatened.

Some scientists think that Hypsilophodon may have eaten insects and small reptiles as well as plants. When it was bending down to eat, Hypsilophodon could have used its short front legs for balance and to grasp food. It had five fingers on its hands and four toes on its feet, which is a lot, since its relatives had only four fingers and three toes!

Like modern gazelles or deer, this fleet-footed little dinosaur lived in herds and relied on high-speed sprints to escape from predators.

THE ESCAPE ARTIST AWARD GOES TO HYPSILOPHODON

Hypsilophodon weighed about the same as a large dog or a small person.

With its long, flexible legs, Hypsilophodon may have been able to race along as fast as a modern-day ostrich.

Hypsilophodon had no problem eating tough plants because its ridged cheek teeth were self-sharpening—what a useful little trick!

In between Hypsilophodon's ribs were plates of gristly cartilage. These plates may have helped to separate the ribs when Hypsilophodon was running fast, so its lungs could expand widely to breathe in lots of oxygen.

Hypsilophodon had large eyes to watch out for danger.

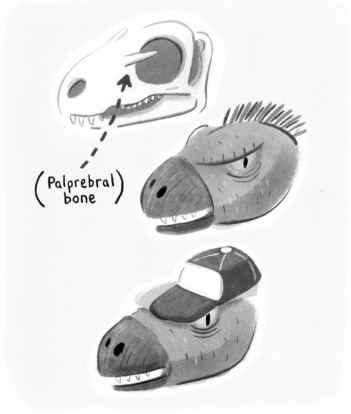

(Palprebral) bone

Thin pointed bones formed protective caps over Hypsilophodon's eyes, making it look as if it was wearing two baseball caps!

When it was running, Hypsilophodon probably kept its spine horizontal and level with the ground. Its long tail was held stiffly off the ground for balance and to stop it from toppling over.

EUOPLOCEPHALUS

How to say the name:
YOO-oh-plo-KEFF-ah-luss
Meaning: well-armored head
When it lived:
76–70 MYA Cretaceous Period

Found in: North America
Diet: low-growing plants, such as ferns and horsetails
Length: 19–23 ft
Height: 6 ft 6 in
Weight: 2 tons

Euoplocephalus was one hefty dinosaur. It was weighed down by its thick, armored coat and heavy tail club, which it would swing like a medieval mace.

Euoplocephalus usually plodded along slowly on its four stumpy legs. If it was angry, it may have charged at full speed, but you'd still be able to outrun it. Euoplocephalus had a broad, toothless muzzle to pull leaves from plants, cheek pouches to store food, and small, ridged teeth to grind plants into a tasty pulp.

Euoplocephalus was probably a loner, rather than a herd animal. The bony shields and spikes on its head, neck, back, and sides would have protected it from attack by predators. It did have a soft and vulnerable belly though, like a porcupine. If a predator managed to flip a Euoplocephalus onto its back, it could rip open its belly—not a pleasant thought…

To avoid this happening, Euoplocephalus relied on a deadly weapon—a hefty tail club made from chunky pieces of bone. This could shatter the teeth or leg bones of an enemy and knock them off their feet.

The **QUEEN OF THE SWINGERS** *Award*

Euoplocephalus was one of the "armored dinosaurs"—dinosaurs with a skin covered in bony plates, like a suit of armor. It was closely related to Ankylosaurus.

THE QUEEN OF THE SWINGERS AWARD GOES TO EUOPLOCEPHALUS

Euoplocephalus's tail club worked a bit like the solid, fixed end of a hammer. The bendy top part of the tail swung the hammer into action when danger threatened.

The nose passages of Euoplocephalus had lots of twists and loops, something like a novelty straw! No one is quite sure what these were for. They may have given Euoplocephalus a good sense of smell.

The large spikes and bony slabs on Euoplocephalus's tablelike back would have made it difficult for predators to bite into.

One of the most heavily armored of all the dinosaurs, Euoplocephalus even had bony eyelids, which flipped down like shutters to protect its eyes.

With a brain small enough to fit inside a teacup, Euoplocephalus was not the brainiest dinosaur on the planet!

Euoplocephalus may have used its tail club to bash into the sides of enemies.

Pardon me!

A huge, barrel-shaped gut probably helped Euoplocephalus to digest its tough plant food, although it would have produced lots of gas—stinky!

MAIASAURA

How to say the name:
MY-ah-SORE-rah
Meaning: Good mother lizard
When it lived:
80–75 MYA Cretaceous Period

Found in: North America
Diet: woody plants, leaves, berries
Length: 29 ft 6 in
Height: 6–8 ft
Weight: 2–4 tons

This devoted dinosaur thoroughly deserves her award for being the world's best dinosaur mom! She was the first dinosaur fossil to be found with her eggs, nests, and young.

Maiasaura nested in large groups, probably so they could warn each other of danger and help to defend their nests and young from attack. They also returned to the same nest site (called "Egg Mountain!") year after year, much as penguins do today.

Maiasaura moms were very busy! They laid a clutch of 30–40 eggs every year. The eggshells were hard and brittle, like those of modern birds. Since Maiasaura laid so many eggs, each one was about the size of a grapefruit.

Although Maiasaura babies hatched out small, they grew up fast. In their first year, they grew from about 1 ft to just over 3 ft long. While they were growing up, they stayed in the herd, where there were plenty of eyes to watch over them. Like other dinosaurs with wide, ducklike snouts (known as duck-billed dinosaurs), Maiasaura probably lived for about 10 years.

The MOM-OF-THE-ERA Award

Maiasaura lived in enormous herds many thousands strong, possibly making long journeys together with the changing seasons to find enough plants to eat.

THE MOM-OF-THE-ERA AWARD GOES TO MAIASAURA

Maiasaura was the first dinosaur in outer space! Astronauts took a Maiasaura eggshell and a piece of bone into space in 1985.

Maiasaura was one chunky dinosaur. It weighed as much as a big male hippo!

We know what Maiasaura liked to munch on thanks to its fossilized poop, which contains the remains of tough, woody plants.

Maiasaura built crater-shaped nests out of mud and arranged the eggs in layers. A covering of rotting vegetation gave off heat and helped the eggs to develop.

Maiasaura's front legs were shorter than its back legs. It probably walked on all fours, but could stand up on its strong back legs to watch out for danger or spot mates and rivals.

Maiasaura had a short, chunky tail, which helped it to balance when it ran along on its back legs at speeds of perhaps 25 mph.

Maiasaura's head was shaped a bit like a horse's head. It had a stout, bony crest near its eyes, which was probably used for showing off to mates or head-butting rivals.

DEINONYCHUS

How to say the name:
Die-NON-i-kuss
Meaning: terrible claw
When it lived:
120–110 MYA Cretaceous Period

Found in: North America
Diet: plant-eating dinosaurs
Length: 10 ft
Height: 5 ft
Weight: up to 165 lbs

Deinonychus was something of an over-achiever. Its brain was much bigger than other similar dinosaurs and it had keen senses of sight and smell, making it a lethal and impressive hunter.

Deinonychus might have lived and hunted in packs, a bit like wolves do today. Working together, these intelligent, agile dinosaurs could have used their brain power to communicate, plan attacks, and overcome giant plant-eating dinosaurs much larger than themselves, such as Tenontosaurus (one of the duck-billed dinosaurs).

As well as being a bit of a brainiac, Deinonychus had a terrifying weapon to help it to kill its prey. On the second toe of each back foot was a huge, curved claw, which was up to 5 in long. When it was walking or running fast on its two strong back legs, Deinonychus held this "terrible" claw off the ground. This stopped the claw from becoming blunt so it was always super-sharp, ready to rip open the soft flesh of its prey, or to fight predators. Deinonychus's long, stiff tail helped it to balance and make quick turns suddenly when chasing its prey. All in all—not one to mess with!

The **TOP OF THE CLASS** *Award*

If there had been a school for predators back in dinosaur times, then Deinonychus—with its big brain and many talents—would have been Top of the Class!

THE TOP OF THE CLASS AWARD GOES TO DEINONYCHUS

Deinonychus was about as long as a car.

It had powerful jaws with more than 60 jagged teeth.

Deinonychus was closely related to Velociraptor, but was almost twice its size.

A pack of *Deinonychus* might have worked together to take down much larger prey. Their large eyes may have helped them to spot their victims.

Deinonychus stabbed its prey with huge claws on its back feet. These claws could suddenly swivel in an arc through 180° to make deep, painful wounds at least 3 ft long.

No evidence of feathers has been found on *Deinonychus* skeletons so far. However, since its cousins, such as *Velociraptor*, did have feathers, it is likely that *Deinonychus* also had feathers for keeping warm, or possibly for display.

Modern-day birds of prey such as eagles and falcons share some characteristics with *Deinonychus*, including speed, agility, large brains, and deadly claws.

The DRAGON SHIELD Awards

We are very pleased to announce the winners of the awards for the dinosaurs with the most awesome and over-the-top body armor! From built-in protective shields and chain mail to stupendous spikes and bony neck rings, these armored dragons were well prepared for anything life might throw at them.

ANKYLOSAURUS (An-KYE-low-SORE-us)
The Armored Tank Award

Length: up to 33 ft; **Weight:** 4.5 tons
When it lived: 74–67 MYA Cretaceous Period
Found in: North America

Built like a tank and covered in rows of bite-proof bony plates like a modern alligator, Ankylosaurus had little to fear from most predators. Its brain was surrounded by a very strong skull, and horns and plates protected its vulnerable eyes.

PINACOSAURUS (PIN-ak-oh-SORE-us)
The Chain Mail Award

Length: 16 ft 4 in; **Weight:** up to 2 tons
When it lived: 80–75 MYA Cretaceous Period
Found in: Asia (Mongolia, China)

The lumps of bone embedded in the skin of Pinacosaurus were like the suits of chain mail armor knights wore into battle in the olden days. Pinacosaurus also had a bony ring around its neck as an extra defense against the sharp teeth or ripping claws of predators.

SAUROPELTA (SORE-oh-PELT-ah)
The Shoulder Spines Award

Length: 16 ft 4 in; **Weight:** 2 tons
When it lived: 121–94 MYA Cretaceous Period
Found in: North America

Sauropelta had two rows of sharp spikes on each side of its neck, which was one of the most vulnerable areas of its body. The spikes would have made this armored dinosaur look bigger and more dangerous, which helped it to intimidate its enemies and bluff its way out of a fight. This was important as it was a slow-mover and did not have a bony tail club to use as a weapon.

GASTONIA (GAS-toe-NEE-ah)
The Awesome Armor Award

Length: 15 ft; **Weight:** 1 ton
When it lived: 142–127 MYA Cretaceous Period
Found in: North America

With so many spikes, it would have been difficult for a predator to jump on to Gastonia's back or sides. As well as its body armor, Gastonia also had a solid shield of armor covering its hips. Like its armored relatives, Gastonia's only weakness was its soft belly. So long as it stayed standing upright, it had a good chance of surviving an attack.

SUCHOMIMUS

How to say the name:
SOOK-oh-MIME-us
Meaning: crocodile mimic
When it lived:
121–112 MYA Cretaceous Period

Found in: North Africa
Diet: Fish, aquatic reptiles, other dinosaurs
Length: 36–39 ft
Height: 9–13 ft
Weight: 3–6 tons

With its long, narrow, tooth-filled snout, Suchomimus looked a little like a dinosaur dressed up as a crocodile for a costume party!

Lining Suchomimus's narrow jaws were about 100 pointed, cone-shaped teeth, which curved backward and were well suited for gripping slippery fish. Huge claws on its thumbs would probably have been used to spear fish, or slash and kill smaller dinosaurs. Suchomimus lived in the same area as gigantic crocodiles, such as Sarcosuchus, and probably competed with these massive prehistoric beasts for food. It may have also scavenged for easy meals by feeding on any dead bodies lying around.

This fierce predator lived in Africa, roaming coastal rivers and lakes in the area that is now the Sahara Desert. Surprisingly, this area was a lot wetter and full of lush green plants in dinosaur times! Suchomimus had strong, tall spine bones on its back. These may have supported a hump, which could have been used to store food. Alternatively, the spines may have supported a sail made of skin, which could have helped Suchomimus to control its body temperature.

The **BEST COSTUME** *Award*

Suchomimus was much smaller than its cousin Spinosaurus, but it would still have towered over a person, who would have only come up to its knees!

Oh no! I didn't know it was a costume party

What do you mean? Your crocodile costume is awesome!

So realistic—where did you get it?

Um...

It's homemade!

Suchomimus may have used its two powerful back legs and its long tail for swimming.

Suchomimus may have been able to swim and hunt for its food in the water.

Beware of the bladelike thumb claws of Suchomimus—they were about 1 ft long! They curved out of the end of thumbs that were even longer, about 1 ft 3 in long…

Suchomimus's long snout ended in a big chin, which held the longest teeth. These teeth could be used to grab and tear apart a really big fish.

PACHYRHINOSAURUS

How to say the name:
PACK-ee-RINE-oh-SORE-us
Meaning: thick-nosed lizard
When it lived:
76–74 MYA Cretaceous Period

Found in: North America
Diet: palms, cycads
Length: 19–23 ft
Height: 10 ft
Weight: 2–3 tons

Pachyrhinosaurus was a champion fighter, with built-in defenses. With a head covered in big bony bumps, called "bosses," as well as horns and spikes, this is one dinosaur you wouldn't want to mess with!

Pachyrhinosaurus had a bulging nose a bit like a boxing glove to help it survive contests with rivals. This nose bump was made of a thick lump of spongy bone. It also had smaller lumps and bumps above each eye. These bony bosses were useful for absorbing the impact of pushing and shoving during fights. A short bony frill helped to protect Pachyrhinosaurus's neck from predators and may also have helped to regulate its body temperature. The frill was usually decorated with a few snazzy-looking horns and spikes, which could injure any predators that did try to attack.

Since Pachyrhinosaurus lived and traveled in large herds, it was also protected from predators by sheer numbers. Some of these herds may have contained hundreds or even thousands of individuals and may have migrated each year. Surprisingly, these chunky dinosaurs could probably run faster than an average dog today, which was another useful form of defense.

The
**DEADLY
DEFENDER**
Award

Thick horns and heavy skull bones allowed Pachyrhinosaurus to bash heads with rivals without turning its brain to mush!

THE DEADLY DEFENDER AWARD GOES TO PACHYRHINOSAURUS

Pachyrhinosaurus was about the same length as a big saltwater crocodile—the largest of all modern-day reptiles.

Pachyrhinosaurus was a plant-eater, tearing off leaves and shoots with its toothless, jagged, parrotlike beak.

Farther back in its mouth, this dinosaur had sharp cheek teeth, which it used for chewing its food.

During duels with rival males, Pachyrhinosaurus butted heads and whacked their strong heads into each other's sides, often breaking ribs in the process.

The winners of these head-to-head contests gained a dominant position in the herd and the right to mate with the females.

Pachyrhinosaurus was a relative of Triceratops. But it had a thick bump on its nose instead of a nose horn.

SAUROPOSEIDON

How to say the name:
SORE-oh-po-SIDE-on
Meaning: earthquake god lizard
When it lived:
110 MYA Cretaceous Period
Found in: North America

Diet: leaves of conifers and flowering trees, such as magnolias, palms, and sycamores
Length: 98–112 ft
Height: 59–66 ft
Weight: 60–80 tons

Named after Poseidon, the Greek god of earthquakes, mighty Sauroposeidon would have made the ground shake with its thunderous footsteps.

Sauroposeidon was a veggie dinosaur, which grew fast and used up energy even faster. This meant it needed lots of plant food to fuel its enormous body. Its long neck helped it to snap up leaves high in the tree tops, which were impossible for smaller plant-eating dinosaurs to reach. To save energy, it would stand still and use its neck to move its head quickly from one tree to the next, munching nonstop.

Sauroposeidon could probably lift its neck up to heights of 55 ft or more, relying on strong neck muscles and air sacs to keep blood flowing and air moving inside its stretched-out neck.

Its towering height would have helped it to spot danger from a long way away. The huge size of an adult Sauroposeidon would also have protected it from most nasty predators. After all, who wants to be squished in the pursuit of dinner?

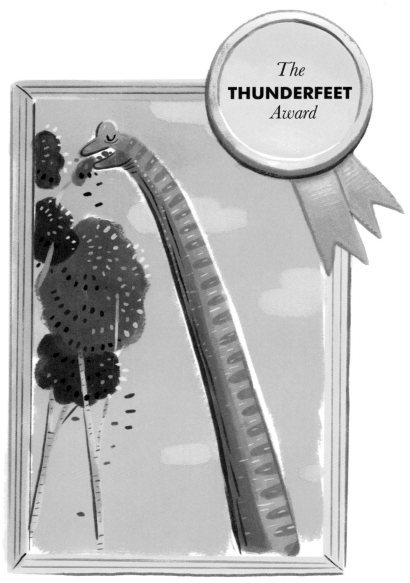

The **THUNDERFEET** *Award*

One of the last of the long-necked dinosaurs in North America, this supersized monster was tall enough to peer through a sixth-floor window.

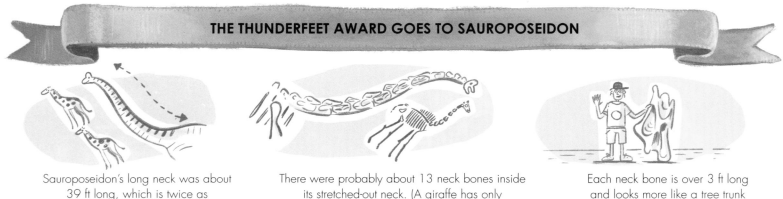

THE THUNDERFEET AWARD GOES TO SAUROPOSEIDON

Sauroposeidon's long neck was about 39 ft long, which is twice as tall as a giraffe.

There were probably about 13 neck bones inside its stretched-out neck. (A giraffe has only seven neck bones.)

Each neck bone is over 3 ft long and looks more like a tree trunk than a bone!

Its small head was also lightweight and housed a very little brain!

Sauroposeidon's four trunklike legs and chunky body provided a strong and stable platform to support its extremely long neck.

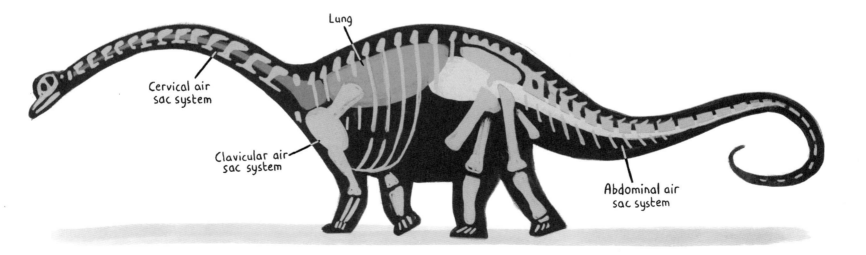

Lung

Cervical air sac system

Clavicular air sac system

Abdominal air sac system

Sauroposeidon was able to breathe enough air because its lungs were very efficient. It also had lots of big air sacs to take in plenty of oxygen from the air, like modern birds. Sauroposeidon's neck was not as heavy as you might think because its neck bones were full of air.

PACHYCEPHALOSAURUS

How to say the name:
PACK-ee-KEF-ah-low-SORE-us
Meaning: thick-headed lizard
When it lived:
76–65 MYA Cretaceous Period

Found in: North America
Diet: leaves, nuts, fruits, insects
Length: 16–26 ft
Height: 6 ft 5 in
Weight: 0.5 tons

Did this dinosaur wear a crash helmet or was it just a fashion diva with some fancy headgear designed for showing off? This is not an easy question to answer!

Pachycephalosaurus is the largest bone-headed dinosaur we know of so far. An adult Pachycephalosaurus had a bony dome about 10 in thick on top of its skull. This is at least 20 times thicker than regular dinosaur skulls. Some fossils have evidence of injuries, which could suggest that rivals bashed their heads together in fights. The thick bony "safety helmet" of a Pachycephalosaurus would have helped to protect its brain. Rivals might also have head-butted each other in the sides rather than crashing into each other head-on. Angry male giraffes fight like this today. As Pachycephalsaurus's domed head was decorated with spikes and bumps, another theory is that Pachycephalosaurus simply used it to impress and woo potential mates.

Pachycephalosaurus probably lived in herds and used its keen eyesight and good sense of smell to keep away from predators. It had strong back legs and a stiff tail for balance, but couldn't run very fast.

The **SAFETY FIRST** *Award*

Pachycephalosaurus lived at the same time as T. rex and Triceratops in North America, just before the dinosaurs died out.

A human skull is only about 7 mm thick, which is over 35 times thinner than the skull of this helmet-headed dinosaur.

The skull of Pachycephalosaurus was made of a special type of bone, which healed rapidly.

Young Pachycephalosaurus individuals may have eaten some meat, such as insects, as well as plants because they had sharp triangular teeth at the front of their mouth.

The broad, leaf-shaped teeth of Pachycephalosaurus suggest that it ate plants. It also had a large gut, which would have helped it to digest tough plants.

STEGOSAURUS

How to say the name:
STEG-oh-SORE-us
Meaning: roofed lizard
When it lived:
155–145 MYA Jurassic Period

Found in: North America, Europe
Diet: ferns, cycads, horsetails, conifers
Length: 19–29 ft
Height: 9–13 ft
Weight: 3–4 tons

One of the most famous dinosaurs of all time, Stegosaurus is easy to recognize from the two rows of leaf-shaped plates, which stood upright like castle battlements along its neck, back, and tail.

The biggest of these plates were almost 2 ft wide and 2 ft tall—that's twice as tall as this book you're reading! They were attached to Stegosaurus's thick skin, not joined to its skeleton. Although they look quite sturdy and spiky, the plates were actually rather thin and fragile. They also had blood vessels running through them and might have changed color when flushed with blood. Some scientists think that the plates were used to flirt with mates or intimidate rivals. Others think that the plates may have acted as giant radiators to help Stegosaurus warm up or cool down.

Another famous feature of Stegosaurus was the 3-foot-long bony spikes at the end of its tail. By whipping this wicked weapon from side to side, Stegosaurus could inflict some seriously nasty injuries on predators.

The
WALKING CASTLE
Award

Stegosaurus's brain was only about the size of a dog's brain, even though "Steggie" was about 100 times larger than a dog.

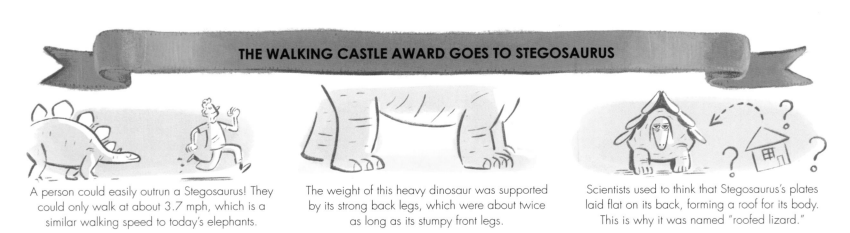

THE WALKING CASTLE AWARD GOES TO STEGOSAURUS

A person could easily outrun a Stegosaurus! They could only walk at about 3.7 mph, which is a similar walking speed to today's elephants.

The weight of this heavy dinosaur was supported by its strong back legs, which were about twice as long as its stumpy front legs.

Scientists used to think that Stegosaurus's plates laid flat on its back, forming a roof for its body. This is why it was named "roofed lizard."

STEGGIE

COUSIN ANKY

Stegosaurus had bony scales to protect its neck, sides, and legs. It was a cousin of the armored dinosaurs (dinosaurs with a skin covered in protective bony plates), such as Ankylosaurus.

Cheek pouches allowed Stegosaurus to store plants while its teeth were grinding up its latest meal. Its teeth were only the size of your little fingernail!

DELICIOUS Stones DINER

Stegosaurus also swallowed stones to help it grind up plants inside its large gut, a bit like a prehistoric liquidizer.

Stegosaurus probably lived on its own or in small groups. It shared the Jurassic woodlands and river floodplains with other famous dinosaurs, such as Diplodocus.

The MARVELOUS MUSIC Awards

Let the trumpets sound and the drum rolls begin... It's time to celebrate four musically-gifted dinosaurs. They might not have been able to work a karaoke machine, but they could honk, bellow, and boom, and we think that deserves some attention!

PARASAUROLOPHUS (Para-SORE-oh-LOAF-us)
The Loudest Trumpeter Award

Length: 36 ft; **Weight:** 2–3 tons
When it lived: 76–74 MYA Cretaceous period
Found in: North America

The huge bony head crest of a Parasaurolophus had tubes inside, through which air from its nostrils could move up and down. The long crest probably worked like a trumpet, to make powerful, low, booming calls, a bit like an elephant trumpeting loudly by pushing air through its trunk.

EDMONTOSAURUS (Ed-MON-toe-SORE-us)
The Singing Seal Award

Length: 29–42 ft 8 in; **Weight:** 3–5 tons
When it lived: 76–65 MYA Cretaceous Period
Found in: North America

One of the last dinosaurs to exist on our planet, Edmontosaurus had large, hollow nostrils, which may have been covered with loose skin. Perhaps this skin could be inflated with air like a balloon to make their bellowing calls louder and warn others of danger, threaten a rival, or attract a mate. The loudspeaker nose of a male elephant seal works in a similar way today.

LAMBEOSAURUS (Lam-BEE-oh-SORE-us)
The Honking Head Award

Length: 30–50 ft; **Weight:** 4–5 tons
When it lived: 76–74 MYA Cretaceous Period
Found in: North America

Lambeosaurus's strange head crest looked a bit like the dinosaur had an ax embedded in the top of its head! The hollow chambers inside the crest would have made this dinosaur's honks louder and able to travel long distances. The crest began as a small bump and grew larger with age. The different shapes and patterns of the crest probably helped individuals recognize each other and find a mate.

CORYTHOSAURUS (Koe-RITH-oh-SORE-us)
The Greek Chorus Award

Length: 32 ft 10 in; **Weight:** 4–5 tons
When it lived: 76–74 MYA Cretaceous Period
Found in: North America

Corythosaurus means "helmet lizard" and this dinosaur was named after its rounded, semicircular head crest, which looks like the helmet of an Ancient Greek soldier. Scientists have made 3D models of Corythosaurus's hollow head crests and found that they create booming sounds when air is blasted through them. Corythosaurus probably used its head crest to signal loudly to its friends. Delicate ear bones, along with a large area of the brain dedicated to hearing, indicate that this dinosaur had a keen sense of hearing.

TROODON

How to say the name:
TROO-oh-don
Meaning: wounding tooth
When it lived:
76–65 MYA Cretaceous Period

Found in: North America, Asia (China)
Diet: small mammals, birds, reptiles
Length: 6–10 ft
Height: 3 ft
Weight: 88–110 lbs

With bigger eyes than most dinosaurs, Troodon didn't need to wear glasses to see well. Its huge peepers may have helped it to hunt insects and reptiles at night, or in cold, dark environments.

Troodon's eyes were about 2 in across, which is about as long as your little finger! They pointed forward, like human eyes, helping this dinosaur to judge how far away things were and pounce accurately on its prey. As well as having huge eyes, Troodon had a bigger brain for its size than almost any other dinosaur. It was probably smarter than the average dinosaur, possibly as smart as a modern chicken.

A quick and agile hunter, Troodon chased after its prey on its long, powerful back legs. It had a large, curved claw on the second toe of each foot, which it could use to attack its prey or defend itself from predators. The claw was probably lifted off the ground when Troodon was walking or running to keep it extra sharp. This "killer" claw was similar to those of Velociraptor and Deinonychus and suggests that Troodon was related to these fierce dinosaurs.

The **WHAT BIG EYES YOU HAVE** *Award*

A fast-moving, intelligent little dinosaur, Troodon was like a big version of a modern bird. Unlike a bird, however, it had long, thin arms, with three clawed fingers for grasping food and other objects.

Want to take a closer look?

No need...

I've brought my own!

The size of Troodon's brain compared to its body was similar to that of today's emus and ostriches.

Troodon probably had a good sense of balance, but was not very good at smelling its environment.

The first Troodon fossil to be found was one of its sharp teeth, which had jagged edges. This is why this dinosaur was named "wounding tooth."

Troodon was a small dinosaur. If it was standing next to an adult man, it would only have come up to his waist.

SCIURUMIMUS

How to say the name:
SKYOOR-uh-MIME-mus
Meaning: squirrel mimic
When it lived:
156–151 MYA Jurassic Period
Found in: Europe (Germany)

Diet: insects, small animals, other dinosaurs
Length: 10 ft
Height: 5 ft
Weight: 165 lbs

Although it had a long, bushy tail like a squirrel, Sciurumimus didn't go around raiding bird feeders and burying acorns! It was a meat-eating menace, and it was covered in fuzzy feathers.

The only Sciurumimus fossil scientists have found so far is of a young, or juvenile, dinosaur, which was not fully grown. It was only about 2 ft long, but scientists think an adult Sciurumimus may have grown as long as 10 ft, based on the size of some of Sciurumimus's relatives such as Deinonychus. The adults may have hunted other dinosaurs, while the tiny juveniles were agile predators of insects and small animals. Sciurumimus would have run fast on two legs to catch its prey and had slender pointed teeth to snap up its meals.

The juvenile Sciurumimus had baby teeth and big eyes. But despite its cute and fluffy appearance, juvenile Sciurumimus was still a fierce little predator, capable of giving a nasty nip.

The **BUSHY TAIL** *Award*

Sciurumumus was a dinosaur predator with a hairlike feathery coat. It was named after its bushy squirrel-like tail.

THE BUSHY TAIL AWARD GOES TO SCIURUMIMUS

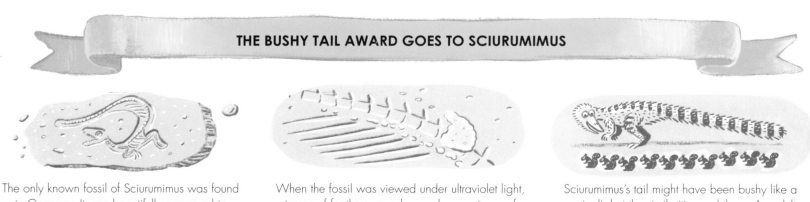

The only known fossil of Sciurumimus was found in Germany. It was beautifully preserved in 150-million-year-old limestone rocks.

When the fossil was viewed under ultraviolet light, traces of feathers, muscles, and even pieces of yellow skin could be seen.

Sciurumimus's tail might have been bushy like a squirrel's but the similarities end there. An adult Sciurumimus may have been as long as about 10 squirrels!

Sciurumimus's feathers may have been downy like those of a baby chick, or shaggy and untidy like those of a modern kiwi or cassowary.

The feathers helped to keep Sciurumimus warm and were not used for flying. The fact that Sciurumimus had feathers suggests that many other predatory dinosaurs may also have been covered in them.

The simple, fluffy feathers of Sciurumimus were similar to those of the flying reptiles called pterosaurs, which were close cousins of the dinosaurs.

GALLIMIMUS

How to say the name:
GAL-ee-MIME-mus
Meaning: chicken mimic
When it lived:
74–70 MYA Cretaceous Period

Found in: Asia (Mongolia)
Diet: insects, plants, fruit, seeds, eggs
Length: 19–26 ft
Height: 11 ft
Weight: 440–992 lbs

Looking somewhat like a big ostrich with a long tail, Gallimimus was a speedy dinosaur that could probably run at speeds of up to 50 mph—that's faster than a modern-day racehorse!

Gallimimus ran very quickly on its strong back legs, using its long tail to balance the weight of its body. Its hollow bones helped to reduce its weight and allowed it to race away from predators, including other dinosaurs. It may also have run around in herds for extra safety. Gallimimus had large eyes, so probably had good eyesight. Its eyes were set high up on the sides of its narrow head, so it could watch all around for danger.

Scientists are not sure what Gallimimus ate, but it may have had a varied diet, feeding on insects, plants, and eggs with its toothless beak. Its hands were like shovels and may have been used to dig up food, such as dinosaur eggs buried in the soil. The long claws on its hands would have been useful for grasping and holding food and possibly pulling down branches or catching small prey, such as worms and lizards.

Even though its name means "chicken mimic," Gallimimus was a lot bigger than a chicken. In fact, it weighed at least 80 times more than a chicken!

THE SPEEDY RACER AWARD GOES TO GALLIMIMUS

Gallimimus had long legs, a long neck, and a long, toothless beak. It also probably had feathers covering its body.

Gallimimus weighed as much as a grand piano and was twice as tall as an adult man.

This dinosaur had a tiny brain, about the size of a golf ball.

Comblike ridges on Gallimimus's beak may have been used to filter food from the water, like ducks do today. Another idea is that these ridges may have been used like a turtle's beak to grasp and pull leaves from plants.

Some of the bones in Gallimimus's beak and lower jaw were paper-thin. They were only a few millimeters thick!

Gallimimus could not see in 3D, because its eyes faced sideways not forward. This position is similar to the eyes of plant-eating animals today. Hunting animals usually have eyes that face forward.

THERIZINOSAURUS

How to say the name:
THER-ee-zine-oh-SORE-us
Meaning: scythe lizard
When it lived:
85–70 MYA Cretaceous Period

Found in: Asia (Mongolia)
Diet: probably plants, possibly insects
Length: 33 ft
Height: 9–16 ft 5 in
Weight: 3–5 tons

This weird and wonderful dinosaur would have been quite a sight. It was about three times taller than an adult human, pot-bellied, and had gigantic, swordlike claws.

Scientists think Therizinosaurus's enormous claws may have been used to pull leafy branches down into its beak. They might also have been used for defense against predators. And it's even possible the massive claws were useful for ripping open termite mounds, like the giant claws of anteaters today.

This dinosaur's wide hips supported its huge barrel-shaped gut, which would have helped Therizinosaurus digest large amounts of plant material. However, this big belly would probably have made Therizinosaurus waddle along slowly and clumsily. Not very dignified!

Scientists haven't yet found a complete skeleton of this curious dinosaur. So, some features, like its teeth, are still a mystery.

Therizinosaurus's claws were each up to about 3 ft long! They are not only the longest dinosaur claws ever found, but also the longest claws of any animal on our planet.

When the first fossilized bones and claws of Therizinosaurus were found, scientists thought they belonged to a giant sea turtle with massive claws, not a dinosaur at all.

Scientists are not sure if Therizinosaurus lived in herds or on its own. But we do know that these dinosaurs nested together, because several fossilized clutches of Therizinosaurus eggs were discovered next to each other.

Therizinosaurus may have been covered in feathers.

Therizinosaurus was far too heavy to fly, so its feathers would only have been used for warmth, or maybe to show off to mates.

OURANOSAURUS

How to say the name:
Oo-RAH-no-SORE-us
Meaning: brave monitor lizard
When it lived:
115–100 MYA Cretaceous Period

Found in: North Africa
Diet: ferns, water plants
Length: 22–26 ft
Height: 10 ft
Weight: 4 tons

As well as the big sail along its back and tail, Ouranosaurus had several other eye-catching features. These included a thumb spike, a ducklike beak, and a long, flat head with two bony bumps in front of its eyes.

Ouranosaurus's sail was supported by a row of long bony rods, which stuck out vertically from its backbone and tail. The sail started growing when Ouranosaurus was about three years old. Its purpose could have been to intimidate rivals, startle enemies, or attract mates. Some scientists think that the sail helped to regulate body temperature or may have stored spare food as fat, like a camel's hump.

The parts of North Africa where Ouranosaurus once lived are dry desert areas today, but 100 million years ago, a lush, swampy tropical forest grew there, crisscrossed by rivers. The broad, toothless beak of Ouranosaurus was good at pulling up lots of soft, leafy water plants. Cheek teeth farther back in its mouth would have been able to mash up these plants before Ouranosaurus swallowed its food. No one is sure if the thumb spikes helped with gathering plants or were used as weapons, or if they were just there to look cool!

The skin on Ouranosaurus's sail may have been brightly colored or even changed color, like a chameleon's skin color changes today—groovy!

THE SUPER SAIL AWARD GOES TO OURANOSAURUS

Ouranosaurus was partly named after a modern-day monitor lizard, which lives in the same parts of Africa that the dinosaur once roamed.

It was as heavy as an Asian elephant.

Its sail was similar to another dinosaur, Spinosaurus, which also lived in Africa a few million years after Ouranosaurus.

SPINOSAURUS

OURANOSAURUS

Nostrils high up on Ouranosaurus's face were less likely to become blocked by mud and dirt while it was feeding on low-growing plants.

Ouranosaurus was a slow-moving, bulky dinosaur that could walk or rest on two or four legs. Its front legs were only half the length of the back legs and its three sturdy middle fingers supported its weight when it rested on all fours.

Ouranosaurus probably ran on its two long back legs to escape predators, such as the giant crocodile Sarcosuchus. Yikes!

The strange bumps on Ouranosaurus's face may have helped it to attract mates, or to recognize its friends and relatives when they were close by.

Unfortunately, they can't be with us today (because they're long extinct!), but please put your hands together and stomp your feet for the four best-dressed dinosaurs of all. These prehistoric award winners sure know how to turn heads with their fab feathers.

ANCHIORNIS (ANK-ee-OR-niss)
The Funky Crest Award

Length: 1 ft; **Weight:** 3.8 oz
When it lived: 160–155 MYA Jurassic Period
Found in: Asia (China)

For Anchiornis there's no such thing as "too much." This chicken-sized dinosaur had a funky crest of orange feathers on its head. It also had downy, gray body feathers and long, black and white feathers on its arms, legs, and tail. It even had feathers on its feet! Its bright head crest probably helped it show off to mates, while its black and white feathers may have been used to dazzle predators, a bit like zebra stripes. Anchiornis probably used its feathers for gliding.

MICRORAPTOR (MIKE-row-rap-tor)
The Four-Winged Flight Award

Length: 2–3 ft; **Weight:** 2 lbs
When it lived: 125–120 MYA Cretaceous Period
Found in: Asia (China)

Microraptor had long, blue-black, shimmering feathers on both its arms and legs, giving it four wings. It could probably glide from trees, or possibly take off from trees, or the ground, for short bursts of flight. Gliding or flying would have helped Microraptor to hunt for small lizards, fish, or mammals, or to escape predators. This birdlike dinosaur shared the skies with early birds and flying reptiles called pterosaurs.

WULONG (WOO-long) and SINOSAUROPTERYX (SINE-oh-SORE-op-ter-ix)

The Pet-Sized Award

Length: 5 ft and 3 ft; **Weight:** 2–3 lbs 3 oz and 5 lbs 5 oz
When they lived: 122–120 MYA Cretaceous Period
Found in: Asia (China)

Would you like to have a pet dinosaur instead of a pet cat or dog? Well, these two award-winning dinosaurs were about the right size (if you ignore their extra-long tails)! Wulong and Sinosauropteryx both had fuzzy feathers, which probably helped them to keep warm. Sinosauropteryx had delicate, chestnut-brown feathers on top and lighter colored feathers underneath. Wulong's extremely long, bony tail with two long, showy feathers at the tip may have been used for signaling to other dinosaurs. Its four wings may have been used for gliding, like its cousin Microraptor.

AVIMIMUS (AH-vee-MIME-us)

The Ostrich Look-Alike Award

Length: 5 ft; **Weight:** 45 lbs
When it lived: 80–70 MYA Cretaceous Period
Found in: Asia (China, Mongolia)

A clever, birdlike dinosaur, Avimimus looked a bit like a modern ostrich. It also ran quickly for long distances on its muscular back legs, at about the same speed as an ostrich. Avimimus's feathers were probably used for keeping warm, for camouflage, or attracting a mate. Its toothless mouth was shaped like a bird's beak for pecking at food. Unlike a bird, however, Avimimus had a bony tail, which would have helped it to balance and steer when zooming along.

DIPLODOCUS

How to say the name:
Dip-LOW-dock-us
Meaning: double beam
When it lived:
155–145 MYA Jurassic Period
Found in: North America

Diet: ferns, cycads, conifers, ginkgo leaves
Length: 88–108 ft
Height: 20 ft
Weight: 22 tons

Diplodocus, aka Dippy, was longer than a tennis court, but most of its extraordinary length was taken up by its super-long neck and even looooonger tail.

Dippy belonged to a group of giant, long-necked, plant-eating dinosaurs called sauropods. It needed huge amounts of plant food to keep its bulky body going and had a massive gut to digest it all. Diplodocus had small, delicate, peglike teeth in the front of its mouth, which were perfect for stripping leaves from tough stalks, a bit like a comb. Each tooth lasted only about 35 days before a new one sprang up to replace it! Dippy didn't have chewing teeth farther back in its mouth so it just gulped down mouthfuls of leaves whole.

Like other sauropods, Diplodocus may have swept its long neck back and forth to scoop up low-growing plants. Its neck contained 15 elongated bones, while its tail—which was longer than a school bus—contained about 80 bones. Dippy's tail was held off the ground and helped to counterbalance the weight of its neck.

The **LONGEST TAIL** *Award*

Scientists think Dippy could whip its tail at supersonic speeds (faster than the speed of sound), producing booming sounds that signaled to friends or frightened off enemies.

Diplodocus had two rows of special bones under its tail. These bones supported the weight of the tail and allowed it to bend easily.

Dippy had broad feet with five toes. One toe on the front legs ended in a large spiky claw, which might have been used for extra grip, for defense, or for feeding.

Inside its head, Dippy had a fist-sized brain. It was certainly not the smartest dinosaur on the block…

Dippy weighed as much as a large truck. It plodded slowly along on its tree-trunk-like legs, at about the walking pace of a human.

OVIRAPTOR

How to say the name:
OH-vee-RAP-tor

Meaning: egg thief

When it lived:
85–75 MYA Cretaceous Period

Found in: Asia (Mongolia)

Diet: fruits, eggs, shellfish, lizards

Length: 6 ft 6 in

Height: 3 ft

Weight: 44–77 lbs

The
**ABSOLUTELY
CRUSHING IT**
Award

Oviraptor may have been toothless, but that never hindered it. This dinosaur simply crushed its food with two bony spikes in the roof of its mouth. In fact, its unusual mouth-gear was probably a useful tool that helped it to crack open eggs, hard fruits, or shellfish.

Oviraptor lived just before the dinosaurs died out, and was a bit of a smarty pants. It had a sharp, curved beak, like a parrot, and was probably covered in fuzzy feathers, like other small, meat-eating dinosaurs alive at the time. Oviraptor's tail was very bendy and muscly, and male Oviraptors might have shaken their colorful tail feathers in a display to attract the ladies. How dreamy!

Oviraptor may have lived in packs, for safety. It used speed to escape from danger, and could run as fast as an ostrich on its long legs. Its three toes had long claws to grip the ground and hold, rip, or tear up its prey. Its hands ended in three long fingers with slender claws, which would have been good at grasping things. Oviraptor may also have snapped its powerful beak together rapidly to intimidate attackers.

If a dinosaur dentist had asked Oviraptor to open its mouth wide, they would have seen no teeth at all! Just two bony points jutting down from the top of its mouth.

THE ABSOLUTELY CRUSHING IT AWARD GOES TO OVIRAPTOR

Oviraptor was named "egg thief" because the first fossils were found near a nest of broken eggs. Scientists thought that Oviraptor was stealing and eating the eggs. However, this was false!

Scientists later found more of the fossilized eggs, which contained the developing embryos of Oviraptor itself.

Soon after that, some amazing fossils of Oviraptor sitting on their nests were found. They had their front legs wrapped around their eggs to protect them. So Oviraptor was not a thief after all!

Oviraptor's large head was sometimes decorated with a helmetlike crest. The crest may have been covered in colored skin and been used to attract a mate or recognize other individuals.

Female Oviraptors laid about 20 eggs at a time, and one or both parents probably took care of the eggs and the baby dinosaurs when they hatched out.

With its lightweight body and long legs, Oviraptor could run very fast over long distances when chasing its prey. It could run faster than most of the other dinosaurs around at the time and change direction with a slight turn of its body.

Big, owl-like eyes on top of a long, bendy neck gave Oviraptor the ability to see predators and prey from long distances all around.

DROMAEOSAURUS

How to say the name:
DROM-ee-oh-SORE-us
Meaning: running lizard
When it lived:
76–74 MYA Cretaceous Period

Found in: North America
Diet: small dinosaurs, lizards, turtles
Length: 6 ft 6 in
Height: 1 ft 7 in
Weight: 33 lbs

A smart, birdlike dinosaur, Dromaeosaurus was a fierce predator, with deadly curved claws on its feet, powerful jaws, strong teeth, and a bone-crunching bite.

About the size of a wolf, Dromaeosaurus may also have hunted in packs, like wolves do today. This would have helped it to catch and kill animals bigger than itself. One of the fastest running dinosaurs, Dromaeosaurus had long back legs and relied on speed to catch its prey. It probably used its huge toe claws to grip its unlucky prey and its powerful jaws to deliver a killing bite. Its long fingers would have been useful for catching and holding thrashing victims. The large, robust teeth of Dromaeosaurus were used for crushing and tearing its food, rather than for slicing through flesh.

Dromaeosaurus had a very stiff tail, which was held straight in an upright position to balance the weight of its body. The tail was flexible near the body, but covered in a lattice of bony rods farther up to keep it straight.

The **BIG BITE** *Award*

With a massive skull and solid jaws, Dromaeosaurus had a bite three times more powerful than that of a Velociraptor.

THE BIG BITE AWARD GOES TO DROMAEOSAURUS

Dromaeosaurus was related to other dinosaurs that had big curved claws on their feet and teeth like daggers, including Velociraptor.

It was named "running lizard" because it was a very speedy runner. It could run as fast as a modern-day coyote.

Dromaeosaurus had such a large brain for its size that for some time scientists thought it had a much bigger body.

Dromaeosaurus held its big toe claws off the ground when it was walking or running. This helped to stop them wearing down and kept them razor-sharp.

Big eyes and excellent vision helped Dromaeosaurus to hunt its prey and watch out for predators. This scary hunter probably also had good senses of smell and hearing.

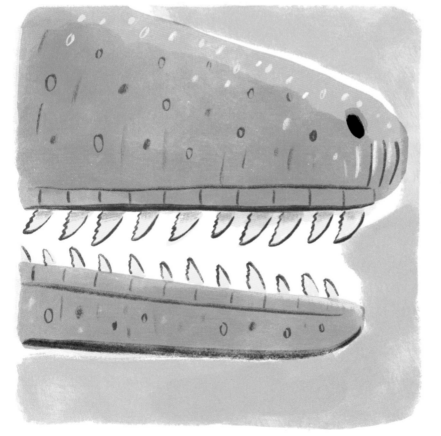

A mouthful of saw-edged teeth pointing backward helped Dromaeosaurus rip flesh off the bones of its prey.

Relatives of Dromaeosaurus had feathers, so it is likely that Dromaeosaurus was also a feathered dinosaur, although no evidence of feathers has been found on its fossils so far.

CRYOLOPHOSAURUS

How to say the name:
Cry-o-LOAF-oh-SORE-us
Meaning: frozen crest lizard
When it lived:
190–170 MYA Jurassic Period
Found in: Antarctica

Diet: other dinosaurs, mammal-like reptiles, mammals
Length: 19–23 ft
Height: 5 ft
Weight: 1,100 lbs

Cryolophosaurus is nicknamed "Elvisaurus" because its off-beat head crest looked a bit like the 1950s quiff hairstyle of rock legend Elvis Presley.

The bony head crest was made from extensions of the skull bones and faced forward, reaching across the head from ear to ear. Its wrinkled surface looked somewhat like a fan or a comb. The crest was too fragile to be used for fighting, so it probably helped to attract mates and may have been brightly colored.

Cryolophosaurus was one of the top predators in the Jurassic world of Antarctica. When Cryolophosaurus was alive, the world's overall climate was warmer and more humid. Antarctica had also drifted about 621 miles farther north, so it was much closer to the warmer area of the Earth around the Equator. This means that Cryolophosaurus was not hunting in a frozen treeless landscape but in cool forests. The trees would have provided perfect cover for Cryolophosaurus to hide and stalk its unsuspecting prey.

The first meat-eating dinosaur to be discovered in Antarctica, Cryolophosaurus was a powerful hunter, with large jaws full of sharp, knifelike teeth.

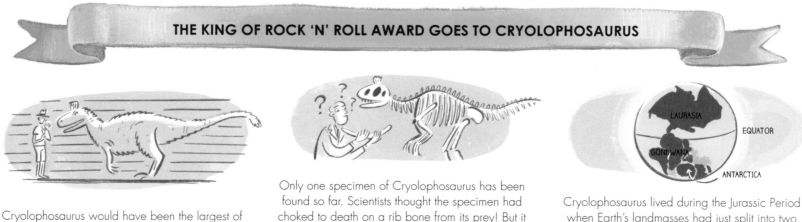

THE KING OF ROCK 'N' ROLL AWARD GOES TO CRYOLOPHOSAURUS

Cryolophosaurus would have been the largest of all the meat-eating dinosaurs in its time.

Only one specimen of Cryolophosaurus has been found so far. Scientists thought the specimen had choked to death on a rib bone from its prey! But it was later realized the rib was the dinosaur's own.

Cryolophosaurus lived during the Jurassic Period when Earth's landmasses had just split into two continents: Laurasia and Gondwana.

With a small brain for its size, *Cryolophosaurus* was not as smart as other large, meat-eating dinosaurs, such as T. rex.

The crest of *Cryolophosaurus* was fixed on both sides to tiny, bony horns above the eyes. The eye horns may have protected the eyes, like bony goggles!

Cryolophosaurus may have been covered in feathers, which would have helped to keep it warm in cool climates.

Large, muscular legs and stout ankles helped *Cryolophosaurus* to run fast, using its long, stiff tail for balance.

INDEX